ANIMALS AND THEIR

Butterflies and Caterpillars

written by Anita Ganeri
illustrated by Anni Axworthy

A⁺
Smart Apple Media

Published in the United States by Smart Apple Media
2140 Howard Drive West, North Mankato, Minnesota 56003

Library of Congress Cataloging-in-Publication Data

Ganeri, Anita, 1961-
Butterflies and caterpillars / by Anita Ganeri.
p.cm. - (Animals and their babies)
Includes index.
ISBN 978-1-58340-808-7
1. Caterpillars—Juvenile literature. 2. Butterflies—Juvenile literature. I. Title.

QL544.2.G345 2007
595.78'139—dc22   2006103528

9 8 7 6 5 4 3 2 1

CONTENTS

A butterfly starts its life as a tiny egg.
A female butterfly lays eggs in spring.
She lays the eggs on plant leaves.

The female lays only one egg at a time, but she can lay as many as 100 eggs a day. She lays her eggs, and then she flies away.

About a week later, the eggs start to hatch. Insi
each egg is a tiny caterpillar.
The caterpillar chews a hole in its eggshell.

Then the caterpillar wiggles out of the hole.
It is hard work to squeeze all the way out.

The caterpillar is hungry!
It munches on leaves.
It uses its jaws to bite
off pieces of the leaves.

The caterpillar is growing fast.
Soon its skin gets so tight
that it splits open.

There is a new, bigger
skin underneath.
The growing caterpillar
changes its skin five times.

When it is three weeks old,
the caterpillar is fully grown.
It is ready to turn into a butterfly.
First, it hangs upside down from a leaf

Then the caterpillar's skin
splits for the last time.
There is a hard case underneath.
This case is called a chrysalis.

Inside the chrysalis, an amazing change takes place. The wiggling little caterpillar turns into . . .

. . . a beautiful butterfly!

It takes about 12 days for the butterfly to grow inside the chrysalis. Then the chrysalis splits open, and the butterfly pulls itself out.

At first, the butterfly's wings are soft and wet.

It holds them in the sun to dry and harden. Now the butterfly is ready to fly away.

Butterflies fly around to find food and places to rest. They also need to fly away from danger. Hungry birds like to eat juicy butterflies.

Butterflies eat a sweet juice from inside flowers. This juice is called nectar. On a sunny, summer day, you might see butterflies flying from flower to flower.

The butterfly pokes its long tongue inside
a flower. Then it starts to slurp! When it
is finished, it rolls its tongue back up.

Next spring, it is time for a male butterfly to meet a female. This is called mating. After mating, the female butterfly lays her eggs on leaves.

Soon tiny caterpillars will hatch out of the eggs. And the caterpillars will turn into . . .

. . . beautiful new butterflies!

Index

Further Information

The butterflies featured in this book are Red Admirals (*Vanessa atlanta*). To find out more about them, you can visit: www.ladywildlife.com/animal/redadmiralbutterfly.html